S0-AUZ-146

3 9114 00030389 5    797.2 PRE
Synchronized swimming is for

# SYNCHRONIZED
# SWIMMING
## is for me

# SYNCHRONIZED SWIMMING
## is for me

Susan Preston-Mauks

photographs by
Karl D. Francetic

 Lerner Publications Company    Minneapolis

The author wishes to thank the following for their assistance in the preparation of this book: The Shaker Heights (Ohio) Board of Education; The Byron Aqua Gems; Sue Berger and the Thornton Park Pool, Shaker Heights, Ohio; Debbi Classen, Andrew K. Deyo, Diane Erickson, Julie Kleinman, Gary Mauks, Leslie Selis, Laura Storms, Stephanie Travill, and Susan Terkel. Special thanks to Carolyn Bruce, who started it all. In memory of Tay Atwell.

**Photos on pp. 7, 9, 14 (top), 35, 36, 37, 38 (top), 41 (left), 43 (bottom), 45 (top), 46 (top) by Julia Sheehan-Burke**
**Photos on pp. 6 (bottom), 7 (top), 19, 31, 38 (bottom), 39, 43 (top), 44, 45 (bottom) by Susan Preston-Mauks**
**Photos on pp. 16, 17, 20 (bottom), 28, 29 by Alice Powers**

*To Kristin and Brandon*

LIBRARY OF CONGRESS CATALOGING IN PUBLICATION DATA

**Preston-Mauks, Susan.**
  Synchronized swimming is for me.

  (A Sports for me book)
  Summary: Sara joins a synchronized swimming class to learn the basics of a sport which combines swimming skills with dancelike moves and fancy stunts performed to music.
  1. Synchronized swimming—Juvenile literature.
[1. Synchronized swimming.  2. Swimming]
I. Francetic, Karl D., ill.  II. Title.  III. Series:
Sports for me books.
GV838.53.S95P73  1983      797.2′1      82-17102
ISBN 0-8225-1139-8 (lib. bdg.)

Copyright © 1983 by Lerner Publications Company

All rights reserved. International copyright secured.
No part of this book may be reproduced in any form whatsoever without permission in writing from the publisher except for the inclusion of brief quotations in an acknowledged review.

Manufactured in the United States of America

International Standard Book Number: 0-8225-1139-8
Library of Congress Catalog Card Number: 82-17102

  2   3   4   5   6   7   8   9   10   92   91   90   89   88   87   86   85   84

Hi! I'm Sara, and one of my favorite sports is synchronized (SINK-ro-nized) swimming. Synchronized swimming is a sport that combines swimming skills with dancelike movements. These movements are put together and performed to music. You **synchronize**, or match, your movements to the beat of the music and to the movements of the other swimmers.

I first became interested in synchronized swimming when I saw my older sister, Kristin, perform in a **swim show** at the recreation center where she takes lessons. A swim show is like a ballet in the water with costumes, colorful lighting, and music. The swimmers were so graceful, and they moved together so perfectly! I decided that I wanted to take lessons, too.

My parents said that I could take lessons, and Kristin's teacher said there was room in her class. There were girls of all ages in the class, and everyone worked at her own pace. Anyone who can swim well in deep water can learn synchronized swimming.

Because the weather was getting nicer, some of our lessons would be held at the indoor pool and some at an outdoor pool.

The next day, I went to the pool with Kristin. She introduced me to Dee Dee, her teacher. Dee Dee explained that many of the skills I would learn are similar to moves learned in gymnastics and dance. Balance, strength, and endurance are all important to synchronized swimming.

Dee Dee said that I would also learn to **modify,** or change, the basic swimming strokes and kicks. The modified kicks help to keep the body high above the water. The kicks and strokes together help you to move through the water in an attractive and graceful way.

Dee Dee explained that the most important synchronized swimming skill I would learn is **sculling**. Sculling is something like rowing a boat. You use your arms and hands like oars.

By pushing and pulling your arms and hands through the water, you can control your body's movement. I would be learning several **sculls**. Some sculls help you to move through the water, and others keep your body in one place.

At my first lesson, Dee Dee taught us the **propulsion sculls**. These sculls **propel**, or move, you through the water. The propulsion sculls are done as you float on the surface of the water on your back, your side, or your front.

Dee Dee demonstrated the basic propulsion scull by first doing it out of the water. You use a strong push-pull motion with the hands and arms. Start with your hands near your hips. The hands and forearms are pulled first towards your body, and then they are brought away from the body. The hands move in figure eights.

We practiced this scull on the pool deck. Dee Dee watched our arm movements carefully to make sure we were doing them right. When she felt we were ready, we jumped into the pool to try the scull in the water.

 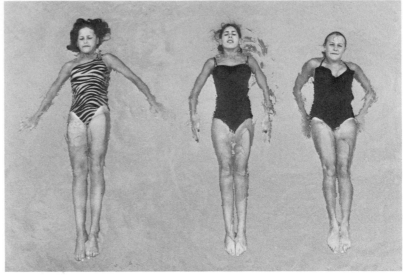

We got in the water, and we practiced floating on our backs with our toes pointed. This is called the **back layout position**. From the back layout position we did the **headfirst propulsion scull** and the **feetfirst propulsion scull.**

To move through the water headfirst, you gently push the water toward your feet. To move through the water feetfirst, you push the water gently toward your head.

At my second lesson, Dee Dee had me do leg stretches and other exercises on the deck. These exercises help stretch and warm up the muscles. Synchronized swimming can be hard work, so it's important to build up strength by exercising.

After we had warmed up, we practiced swimming under water. In synchronized swimming, you often have to stay under water for long periods of time. I knew I would have to work hard to develop good breath control.

At first, I spit out a little water every time I surfaced. That didn't look very nice! So Dee Dee showed me how to blow out air as I surfaced. Then when I reached the surface, I'd be ready to breathe in instead of out.

We practiced holding our breath in shallow water first. Then we did somersaults under water and practiced blowing out bubbles when surfacing. It was much easier doing somersaults in the water than on land. I felt weightless as I turned around in the water. Dee Dee explained that the weightless feeling was caused by my natural **buoyancy** (BOY-yan-see), or ability to float.

The next synchronized swimming skill I learned was the **modified crawl stroke**. I already knew the front crawl, which is done with the face in the water, legs kicking, and rhythmic breathing. For the modified crawl, however, the head is lifted out of the water completely, and the feet are lowered toward the bottom of the pool until you are almost in a standing position. Stroke with your arms as if you were doing the regular crawl stroke. The upper part of the body should be well out of the water. It was hard to do the modified crawl without sinking!

To help keep from sinking, the **eggbeater kick** is used. To do the eggbeater kick, the right leg moves in a counterclockwise circle and the left leg in a clockwise circle. It is like kicking a soccer ball with the inside of your right foot and then with the inside of your left foot. One leg follows the other.

Dee Dee had me sit on the diving board to practice the eggbeater kick. Soon I was able to do it in the water, too. The eggbeater kick is used with several synchronized swimming strokes.

I was happy when Dee Dee said I was ready to learn a **figure**. Figures are the fancy stunts I had seen at Kristin's swim show. They are combinations of different sculls and **body positions**. Body positions are the basic ways to hold the body in the water between moves. There are hundreds of different figures. The one I'd be learning first was the **tub**.

I started in the back layout. Then I brought my knees to my chest and dropped my hips under water. I then started to turn my body around in a circle on top of the water by using the basic propulsion scull. The fingers of my left hand pointed upward, and I pulled that hand toward my body. My right hand was held fingers down, and I pushed that hand away from my body.

With practice, I could do the tub easily. And I soon figured out how to move in different directions by changing hand positions. Doing the tub was really fun!

The next figure I learned was the **ballet leg**. The ballet leg is used with many different movements for other figures, too. You need a strong scull to do the ballet leg.

Dee Dee showed us the ballet leg. She started in the back layout position and used the figure-eight scull we had learned. But instead of pushing in one direction, she pushed evenly in and out. This scull kept her from moving in any direction. It is called the **stationary scull** and is used when you don't want to move through the water at all.

From the back layout position, Dee Dee bent her right knee toward her chest. This is called the **bent knee position** and is used in many figures. From this position, she raised her leg until it was straight up in the air with the toes pointing toward the ceiling. Next she bent the straight leg back down to the bent knee position and then lowered it until she was in the layout again.

1895 OAK

Dee Dee helped each of us try a ballet leg. It was easy to raise my leg up, but it wasn't easy to stay on top of the water! Now I really understood the importance of sculling and how it helps to keep your body from sinking. The more I practiced the ballet leg, the stronger my scull became.

One day Dee Dee taught us the **vertical position**. In the vertical position, your body is held straight up and down in the water, and your legs extend above the water's surface.

Dee Dee taught us a special scull to use when in the vertical position. This scull is called the **support scull** because it **supports**, or holds, your body above the water.

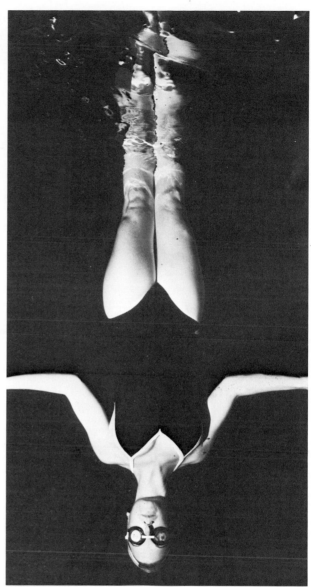

To do the support scull, an even push-pull motion is done with the hands at shoulder level, parallel to the bottom of the pool. First we practiced the support scull in the shallow end of the pool. Then we went to the deep end, turned upside down in the vertical, and practiced it.

My scull wasn't strong enough at first. I kept sinking and tipping over. So Dee Dee helped me find my **center of gravity**. The center of gravity is what keeps a person balanced. In the water, your center of gravity is determined by the position of your hands and body. Dee Dee told me that tight muscles and even sculling would keep me balanced while doing the vertical.

Kristin and I practiced the support scull together. Because Kristin is more buoyant than I am, she could keep more of her body above the water. With practice, though, my scull would become stronger, and I'd be able to do it as well as Kristin.

KNIGHT VARIATION POSITION

You can do other positions from the vertical position. If you bend one knee, for example, you are in the **knight variation position**. If you straighten that leg onto the surface of the water, you are in the **crane position**. The **split position** is done by straightening both legs, one in front of the body and one behind. Dee Dee did these positions for us, and then we tried them.

CRANE POSITION

SPLIT POSITION

After practicing the verticals, we were ready to learn more figures. The figure I enjoyed most is the **dolphin**. I especially liked the **bent knee dolphin.**

The bent knee dolphin is something like a backbend. Your starting position is the back layout. Bring your knee up to your chest. Then arch your back and do a head-first scull.

By keeping your back arched and your head back, you will travel in a large circle under water. You continue the circle until you're back on the surface where you started.

Dee Dee did the dolphin beautifully. Like many older synchronized swimmers who spend a lot of time under water, Dee Dee sometimes wears goggles and a noseclip in the pool.

After a few more weeks of practicing sculling, the eggbeater kick, modified stroking, and the basic body positions, Dee Dee said it was time to learn a **routine** (roo-TEEN).

A routine, she explained, is combining swimming strokes and figures and performing them to music. It's much like doing a dance number on stage, only in synchronized swimming most of the moves are done in the water. We would be learning our routines for a swim show that was coming up in a few weeks.

To show us what a routine would be like, Dee Dee had us practice swimming and doing ballet legs to the beat of the music. Dee Dee then told us that she would **choreograph** (KOR-ee-uh-graf) a routine for each of us. To choreograph a routine, you match movements to the rhythm and mood of the music. The movements are arranged so that they flow together smoothly.

Some of the routines would be performed
by two girls. This is called a **duet**. Routines
with four or more swimmers are called **team
routines**. A routine performed by just one
swimmer is called a **solo.**

Dee Dee told Kristin that she would be swimming in two duets with Katie, another girl in the class. Kristin and Katie got to choreograph one of their routines and choose their own costumes. I would be in a team routine choreographed by Dee Dee. I was thrilled when she told me I would have a short solo at the end!

We learned our routines by practicing on the pool deck first. That way we could practice them many times without getting tired. When we knew our routines well, we would try them in the water.

The swim show was only a few weeks away, so we all worked very hard. We also had to choose costumes for our routines. The costumes had to be made of very light-weight material so that they would be easy to swim in. I would be wearing an elf costume. Kristin and Katie chose short skirts and umbrellas for one of their routines.

Finally the day for the swim show arrived. We were all very excited as we put on our costumes and our special waterproof make-up. Dee Dee helped us get ready.

Before the show began, Dee Dee thanked the audience for coming. She told them a little about the show and about synchronized swimming. We stood near the locker room where the audience couldn't see us and listened to what Dee Dee was saying. When she told the audience how hard we had worked, I felt so proud.

The show went very well. My routine was first. I was nervous until I started swimming. Then I forgot about the audience and just had a good time. Kristin and Katie swam their routines beautifully, too.

After the show, I thought about everything I had learned. Synchronized swimming takes a lot of hard work. In fact, many young women are practicing hard for the synchronized swimming competition that will take place at the 1984 Olympics. But the thing I like best about synchronized swimming is that it's lots of fun. I'm glad synchronized swimming is for me!

# SYNCHRONIZED SWIMMING Words

**BACK LAYOUT:** A basic body position done by floating on the back with legs straight and parallel to the surface of the water

**BALLET LEG:** A synchronized swimming figure done with the body in a back layout. One leg is held parallel to the water surface, and the other leg is held straight up, perpendicular to the water.

**BENT KNEE POSITION:** A basic body position. While in the back layout, one knee is brought toward the chest.

**BODY POSITIONS:** The basic ways of holding the body in the water between moves

**BUOYANCY:** The ability to float, determined in humans by body build and lung capacity

**CENTER OF GRAVITY:** The point at which an object is perfectly balanced

**CHOREOGRAPH:** To arrange a series of dance or dancelike moves to music

**DOLPHIN:** A synchronized swimming figure in which the body arches backwards and travels in a circle under water

**DUET:** A routine performed by two swimmers

**EGGBEATER KICK:** A synchronized swimming kick used to keep the upper body above the water's surface

**FEETFIRST SCULL:** A propulsion scull that moves the body through the water in the direction the feet are pointing

**FIGURE:** Fancy stunts performed in the water that are combinations of different sculls and body positions

**HEADFIRST SCULL:** A propulsion scull that moves the body in the direction the head is pointing

**MODIFIED CRAWL:** A synchronized swimming stroke which helps keep the body upright while moving through the water

**SCULLS:** Various hand-and-arm movements used to support and/or move the body through the water

**SOLO:** A routine performed by one person

**SUPPORT SCULL:** A scull used when the body is in an upside-down vertical position. Also called the *sustained height scull.*

**STATIONARY SCULL:** A figure-eight scull which keeps the body in one place in the water

**SWIM SHOW:** A group of synchronized swimming routines performed to music for an audience

**SYNCHRONIZED:** Happening at the same time

**TEAM ROUTINE:** A routine performed by four or more swimmers

**TUB:** A figure in which the body makes a full circle on the water's surface

**VERTICAL:** An upside-down body position

## ABOUT THE AUTHOR

SUSAN PRESTON-MAUKS is involved in physical education and sports as a coach, administrator, teacher, writer, and participant. She has taught and coached synchronized swimming at all age levels and began her own AAU (Amateur Athletic Union) team. Preston-Mauks has worked as a management consultant for sports programs and is assistant director of the Weed Physical Arts Building at Keuka College in Keuka Park, New York, where she is also assistant professor of physical education, specializing in aquatics.

## ABOUT THE PHOTOGRAPHER

KARL D. FRANCETIC graduated from the Rochester Institute of Technology in New York with a degree in photography. Now a commercial photographer, Mr. Francetic's photographs have appeared in many national magazines. He is the owner of Francetic Photo Associates in Miami, Florida.